Epic Deer Adult Coloring Book

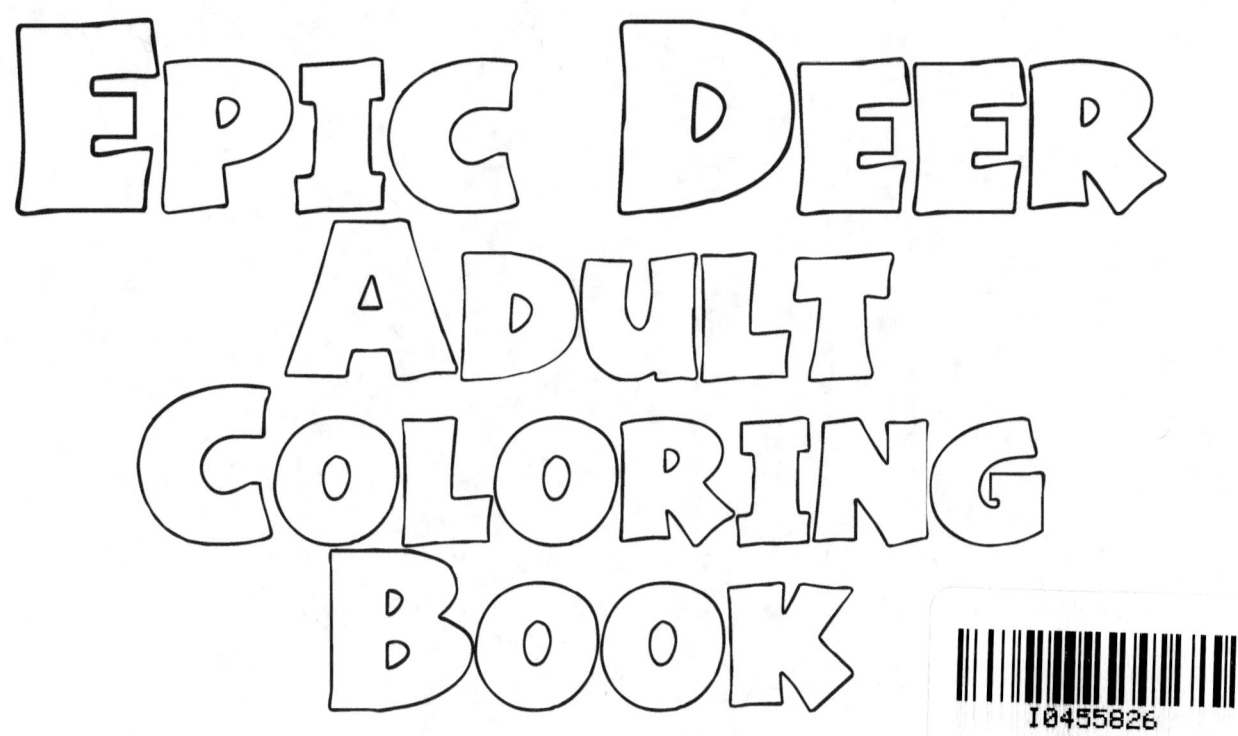

BY SUSAN POTTERFIELDS

Copyright © 2016 Susan Potterfields

ISBN: 10: 1535330244
ISBN-13: 978-1535330244

I0455826

Other Coloring Books By Susan Potterfields

Epic Cat Adult Coloring Book
Epic Dog Adult Coloring Book
Epic Cow Adult Coloring Book
Epic Chicken Adult Coloring Book
Epic Dolphin Adult Coloring Book
Epic Crab Adult Coloring Book
Epic Bear Adult Coloring Book
Epic Turkey Adult Coloring Book
Epic Boar Adult Coloring Book
Epic Sheep Adult Coloring Book
Epic Rabbit Adult Coloring Book
Epic Pig Adult Coloring Book
Epic Fish Adult Coloring Book
Epic Funny Fish Adult Coloring Book
Epic Snack Adult Coloring Book

And Many More